Month-by-Month Write & Read Books

15 Reproducible Predictable Books That Your Students Help Write!

by Veronica Robillard

SCHOLASTIC
PROFESSIONAL BOOKS

New York • Toronto • London • Auckland • Sydney • Mexico City • New Delhi • Hong Kong

Dedication

To Kenneth, Christine, and Kevin, and to the wonderful students I have worked with who have been instrumental in helping me develop this program.

Cover design by Jaime Lucero

Interior design by Ellen Matlach Hassell for Boultinghouse & Boultinghouse, Inc.

Cover and interior illustrations by James Graham Hale, except page 2 by Maxie Chambliss

ISBN 0-590-98360-1

Contents

Month-by-Month Write & Read Books

Introduction

Write & Read Books are a creative and interactive way to teach early literacy skills to children! The first Write & Read book was so well received that I have developed a second book in the series. *Month-by-Month Write & Read Books* take you through the school year with topics such as back to school, seasons, special events, holidays, and more! Using the predictable, patterned story templates, children write and illustrate their own books, which they can then take home and share. Children learn by writing, reading, listening, and speaking. They also learn from the feedback and support of their audience.

As they create their own unique books, children experience success and a sense of ownership. They realize that they can do the writing and the reading. The process is self-nourishing. As children develop confidence, they are motivated to write more and to read what they have written.

The books are both easy to make and easy to use. I usually make a model of each book and share it with the class as I introduce the concept. You'll find suggestions for presenting individual books on pages 5–17. You may want to reproduce the "About the Author" template on page 94 to add to each book.

Children complete the books in keeping with their own literacy development. The amount of direction and instruction depends on children's needs. Preliminary group work on the chalkboard or chart pads is often helpful to get them started. For early learners, I sometimes make dotted-line letters or write letters in fine yellow marker as children dictate the words for their stories. For advanced learners, I encourage a more colorful and detailed text. Illustrating the stories provides children with another way to express their ideas.

The amount of time and the depth of the lessons for each book vary. I encourage you to extend the concepts and ideas to the degree that time, resources, and student needs allow. However you decide to use Write & Read Books, you'll find that they are easy to integrate into your teaching.

A critical component is to provide children with the opportunity and encouragement to read their books again and again—to themselves, to other students, to family members, or to other classes. As they share their books, children learn to use cues such as patterns in the text, high-frequency words, and illustrations to help them become fluent readers.

Each book includes a "Comments" page on the back cover. This page provides a place for family members or classmates to respond to, and to reinforce, the author's efforts with positive comments. You'll find a letter to family members on page 18, which you can duplicate and send home, explaining the importance of this feedback in helping children grow as writers and readers.

I suggest considering a predictable pattern in making and sharing the books. I include them as part of my scheduled routine. We make a book in class each week. Children take their books home every Friday and return them on Monday with responses from family members.

In addition to making the 15 books included here, you and your class may want to write your own stories. Use the templates on pages 95–96 for students' original work.

With Write & Read Books, children, teachers, and parents all join together to foster literacy growth. I think you'll find the experience both rewarding and enjoyable.

Getting Started with Write & Read Books

When introducing a mini-book, it is beneficial to create a completed sample to show the class. By reading through your book and pointing out all the steps you took, you help children feel comfortable when they create their own mini-books.

The books have been designed for ease of assembly. See the detailed instructions below. It is best to assemble the books together as a class. Of course, you might want to assemble the books yourself, depending on the time of year and the level of children.

Assembling the Books

1. Copy the pages for books on standard 8½-inch by 11-inch paper, making the pages single-sided.

2. Fold the front cover/back cover in half along the dashed line, keeping the fold to the left side.

3. Fold each inner page in half, keeping the fold to the right side.

4. Place the inner pages inside the cover and staple three times along the spine.

School Bells Ring

SEPTEMBER pages 19–22

Purpose
Children focus on the transition from summer to the school year. Children review school-related vocabulary.

Strategies for Starting
Talk about the changes from summer vacation to back-to-school routines. Ask: *What was different in your home this morning compared to mornings in the summer? Was there a difference in your after-dinner activities last night compared with before school started? Was your bedtime last night earlier or later than your bedtime before school started? Did you feel different this morning than in the summer?* Invite children to note what else has changed or not changed in their daily routine and lifestyle. Perhaps make a chart comparing things that are different and things that are the same.

Introduce the Book
Display the model book that you made. Read it aloud to the class. Explore other possibilities for filling in the missing words. You may want to brainstorm as a group a list of possible responses for each page. Write children's ideas on the board for children to refer to as they make their books.

Encourage children to personalize their books according to their feelings about the start of the school year.

Make the Book

Duplicate and pass out pages 19–22 of this book. Either preassemble the books or help children assemble their books. Stress the importance of drawing illustrations that match the text. Remind children to include their names on the cover. Refer to the introduction for suggestions on how to support children who need extra help.

Share the Book

Invite children to take turns reading their books aloud to the class. Encourage one-to-one word correspondence. Send the books home along with the letter on page 18. When children return their books, add them to a back-to-school display. The names printed on the front covers will allow children to become familiar with the spelling of one another's names.

Beyond the Book

You may choose to elaborate on these topics:

- forming possessive nouns (such as "My teacher's name is . . .")
- comparing and contrasting (favorite/least favorite)
- deciding what makes something special

....
TEACHING TIP: This book is a great way to get to know about your students at the start of the school year!
....

Autumn

SEPTEMBER pages 23–26

Purpose

Children observe the seasonal changes of autumn.

Strategies for Starting

Talk about the leaves changing color and make a list of autumn color words. Encourage seasonal awareness by asking: *What are the four seasons? What season is it now? What are some of the special features of autumn? What are some of the changes that we observe? What do you like about autumn?*

Introduce the Book

Display the model book you have made. As you read it aloud, emphasize the phrase "I see _____" Let children guess the ends of sentences based on the illustrations. Discuss the meaning of the words *observe* and *observation*. Explain that children will observe the changes that take place during autumn and will record their observations in their books.

Make the Book

Duplicate and distribute pages 23–26 of this book. Either preassemble the books or help children assemble their books. Discuss the relationship of pictures to print. Explain that pictures can be valuable clues to figuring out words. To demonstrate this idea, you could compare a picture book without words and a picture book with simple text and rich illustrations. Explain that the words children write in their books should match the pictures. Invite children to draw a picture of themselves on the cover. On the last page, have them illustrate their favorite part of autumn.

Share the Book

Invite children to share their favorite pages of their books with the class. Send the books home for children to read to family members.

Beyond the Book

Develop children's understanding of autumn by exploring changes in daylight hours and temperature. Compare and contrast earlier to later, warmer to cooler, and so on. Discuss special activities or celebrations that take place in autumn.

TEACHING TIP: Develop an autumn word bank for use in different kinds of writing, such as journals, creative writing, poetry, and scientific exploration. You can then compile student work for a class book about autumn. Try making a book for each season!

Fall Harvest

OCTOBER   **pages 27–30**

Purpose

Children learn about the fall harvest in a patterned, predictable text. Children review vocabulary related to the harvest. Children support text with illustrations.

Strategies for Starting

As a group, brainstorm a list of foods children like to eat in the fall. Then discuss what foods they like to eat during other seasons. Are they different or the same? Ask: *Why might you prefer different foods during different times of the year?* Then discuss how we get our food, especially food that is harvested. Ask: *Who grows fruits, vegetables, and grains? How do they grow them? How does it get to us?*

Introduce the Book

Show children the sample book that you have made. Read aloud the first few pages. Invite children to follow the pattern and join in after you have read the first line of each verse. Repeat until they are familiar with the pattern. Point out the phrase "in the _____." Have children locate that phrase on each page.

Make the Book

Duplicate and pass out pages 27–30 of this book. Either preassemble the books or help students assemble their books. Review the relationship of pictures to print. Point out that students can use clues in the text to help them draw their pictures. On the last page, they can fill the shopping cart with food.

Share the Book

Divide your class into six groups and assign each group a verse. Ask each group to make up a movement to represent the action (or verb) in the verse. Give children time to practice reciting their verse with movement. Then have the groups read their verses in the order of the book, acting out the verbs. Next have the class read the entire book together, with everyone doing all of the movements. Finally, send the books home for children to share with family members.

Beyond the Book

- Make an audiotape recording of students reading the book together. Keep it in a listening center with students' books.
- Make labels for objects in the classroom using the phrase "in the _____" (examples: in the basket, in the closet, in the trash).
- Use the book to introduce a unit on farms and harvesting.

Apples, Apples, Apples

OCTOBER   pages 31–36

Purpose

Children review numbers. Children practice counting backward in a patterned text. Children practice simple subtraction.

Strategies for Starting

Review the numbers 0 to 10. As a group, practice counting backward from 10 to 1, like a rocket countdown. To introduce subtraction, display a group of ten apples (or other objects) in the front of the room. As the class counts backward, remove one apple at a time so that students can see the pile getting smaller.

Introduce the Book

Show children your sample book. Read aloud the first few pages. Invite children to follow the pattern and join in after you read the first line of each page. Then read the book in unison, emphasizing one-to-one word correspondence.

Make the Book

Duplicate and pass out pages 31–36 of this book. Either preassemble the books or help students assemble their books. Ask students to draw the appropriate number of apples in the tree on each page. (For example, students would draw 8 apples for "Eight little apples hanging from a tree.") Then show students how they can cover up one apple and count the other apples to solve the subtraction problem. Point out the lines where they can write their answers. Remind them to write their names on the front covers.

Share the Book

Invite children to read the book in unison. Children may also read the book in pairs, alternating pages. They can use manipulatives while they read to reinforce the concept of subtraction. Have them take their books home to share and get responses from family members.

Beyond the Book

- Study connections between numerals and number words.

- Discuss the use of the question mark and ask students to make up their own sentences using question marks. Demonstrate how a sentence sounds different if it ends in a question mark. Ask them to read their sentences with a questioning intonation.

Tiny Spider

NOVEMBER   pages 37–40

Purpose

Children identify direct quotations. Children identify descriptive words (adjectives).

Strategies for Starting

Ask children where they might find a spider in their homes. Discuss how and why spiders make webs.

Introduce the Book

Share the model book that you made. As you read aloud, give the spider a distinct voice so that students can hear the direct quotations.

Make the Book

Duplicate and pass out pages 37–40 of this book. Either preassemble the books or help students assemble their books. Review the relationship of pictures to print. Ask students to find what the spider says on each page by looking for words inside quotation marks. Then have them copy the quotations into the talk balloons to reinforce the concept. Invite students to draw a picture of themselves on the last page with the spider.

Share the Book

Assign children roles from the book as the different animals and the spider. Encourage children to act out the descriptions of the animals as other students read aloud. For example, the student playing the snake should act out "sneaky" and "slithering." Then send books home for children to share with family members.

Beyond the Book

Introduce adjectives as words that describe people, places, or things. Read the book again, stopping to ask students to describe the animal the spider meets on each page. For example, ask: *What kind of goat did he meet?* (a *grumpy* goat) and *What kind of child did he meet?* (a *cheerful* child) Explain that these words are adjectives. Ask students to think of adjectives that describe other animals beginning with the same letter, such as *happy hippo* or *bashful bat*. List on the board the adjectives they think of. Challenge the class to come up with an adjective and animal for every letter of the alphabet. Then have each student illustrate one animal/adjective combination for a class "animal, adjective, alphabet" book.

TEACHING TIP: Make a spider learning center with books and posters about spiders. Encourage children to write creative stories or reports about spiders; draw or paint spiders using photographs for reference; and create three-dimensional spiders using pipe cleaners, paper rolled into balls, and other materials.

I Am Thankful

NOVEMBER   pages 41–45

Purpose

Children identify what they are thankful for in their lives.

Strategies for Starting

Discuss what it means to be thankful. Invite children to share what they are thankful for. Point out that we sometimes take things for granted and it is good to think about the gifts or blessings in our lives. You may want to connect this book with the celebration of Thanksgiving.

Introduce the Book

Display the model book that you made. Read it aloud to the class. Point out that the sentences begin the same way. Stress one-to-one word correspondence. Explain that the pictures you drew are helpful clues to recognizing the words on each page.

Make the Book

Duplicate and pass out pages 41–45 of this book. Either preassemble the books or help children assemble their books. Invite children to draw a picture of themselves on the cover with something for which they are thankful. Elicit possible responses for each page. Write these on the chalkboard to help children with spelling and vocabulary development. Stress the importance of drawing pictures that support what they have written.

Share the Book

Emphasize that the sentences have a patterned beginning. Invite children to share their books with a partner. Ask for several volunteers to read their books aloud and to share their pictures with the class. Have children bring their books home to read to family members over the Thanksgiving holiday.

Beyond the Book

- Make a bulletin board display featuring a large turkey with colorful cut-out feathers. Have each child create a "feather" for the turkey with the words "I am thankful for _____." Encourage them to fill in the blank with an idea from their book.
- Make a class graph of students' favorite Thanksgiving foods.

One Cold, Snowy Morning

DECEMBER   pages 46–52

Purpose

Children count objects and write numerals. Children review descriptive verb forms ending with -*ing*. Children review characteristics of winter.

Strategies for Starting

Invite children to share observations they might make on a cold, snowy winter day while on their way to school. Ask children to express their responses using -*ing* words, such as "I saw snowflakes falling" or "I saw people shoveling." Whisper different -*ing* verbs for children to act out, such as *sneezing*, *dancing*, *hopping*, *crying*, and *laughing*. Ask other children to guess the verb being acted out.

Introduce the Book

Read aloud the sample book that you made, emphasizing the -*ing* verbs. You can let children take turns counting the number of objects on each page.

Make the Book

Duplicate and pass out pages 46–52 of this book. Either preassemble the books or help children assemble their books. Have children count the number of objects on each page and write a numeral on the blank. On the last page, children can draw a snowy winter scene. Then invite them to color in their books and write their names on the covers.

Share the Book

Have children practice reading their books with expression to a partner. Then ask pairs of partners to identify all of the *-ing* verbs. Invite volunteers to read the book (or parts of the book) expressively while the class acts out the *-ing* verbs. Send home the books for sharing with family members. When the books are returned, they can be added to a winter display.

Beyond the Book

- Ask children to identify the adjectives in the book. Ask: *What kind of snowflakes were falling? What kind of icicles were hanging?* This patterned questioning will help children find the adjectives on their own. Make a list of the adjectives from the book, then have children generate their own adjectives to add to the list.

- Using the templates on pages 95–96, have children work collaboratively to create similar books with titles such as *One Happy Elementary School* or *One Fun-Filled Playground*.

How to Make a Snowman

JANUARY   pages 53–57

Purpose

Children count objects and write numerals. Children recognize sequence words *(first, then, at last)*.

Strategies for Starting

Have children share their experiences with making snowmen. Encourage children to describe the process of building a snowman. Ask children how they would teach a younger friend or sibling to build a snowman, step by step.

Introduce the Book

Display the book that you made as a model. Also emphasize the importance of using clues in the illustrations to help students fill in the appropriate text.

Make the Book

Duplicate and pass out pages 53–57 of this book. Either preassemble the books or help children assemble their books. On page 1, students can draw themselves building a snowman. On pages 2–7, have children count the objects on each page and fill in numerals on the appropriate lines. Finally, invite children to color in the pictures and add details to personalize it. Suggest that on each page they draw themselves building the snowman.

Share the Book

Ask for volunteers to read pages of the book while other students act out what is being read. Send the books home for students to read to family members.

Beyond the Book

- Invite children to write or tell a short story using sequence words. (The story can be their own or one they already know.) You might give them suggestions to start the story, such as "Once upon a time . . ." or "The first thing that happened . . ."

- Ask children to use sequence words as they write or tell instructions for a task that they are experts in, such as making a peanut butter and jelly sandwich or doing a cartwheel.

100 Is Fun to Count

FEBRUARY pages 58–64

Purpose

Children draw 100 objects in ten groups of ten. Children review opposites.

Strategies for Starting

Have students think about how many days they have been in school this year. Review counting to 100 by 10's, 5's, 2's, and 1's. Ask students to think of combinations that equal 100, such as 50 + 50, 99 + 1, and 25 + 25 + 25 + 25. Have them consider how many hundreds, tens, and ones are in 100.

Introduce the Book

Share with the class the sample book that you made. Encourage children to note the correspondence between your drawings and the text. Discuss the concept of opposites and have children generate a list of opposites.

Make the Book

Duplicate and distribute the book. Either pre-assemble the books or help children assemble their books. Discuss what things are hot, cold, big, small, round, square, soft, hard, loud, and quiet. List them on the board for children to refer to as they make their books. Have children draw ten pictures in each category. You may ask them to complete a section of the book each day for several days.

Share the Book

Share and compare the finished books as part of your 100th Day celebration. Send the books home for students to read to family members and friends. When they return the books, display them on a bulletin board titled "Celebrate 100!" before adding them to students' personal libraries.

Beyond the Book

Explore the numbers 1 to 100 with activities in writing, reading, science, math, social studies, art, music, and physical education. Here are some ideas:

- Count 100 kernels of popcorn; then pop and enjoy!
- String 100 pieces of cereal to make a necklace.
- Make a headband with 100 tally marks on it.
- Make student badges that say "I made it to the 100th day of _____ grade!"
- Count 100 steps.
- Read 100 books.
- Graph the colors of 100 colored cubes.
- Make a chart with 100 thumb prints.
- Count 100 raisins; make groups of 2, 5, and 10 before eating!
- Count 100 cents.
- Do 100 math problems.
- Spend an imaginary 100 dollars.
- Sort 100 shells, buttons, beans, or other small objects.
- Write a story with 100 words.
- Make a design or picture with 100 toothpicks.
- Make a list of 100 words students can read.
- Display collections of 100 objects.

If I Were President

FEBRUARY   pages 65–68

Purpose
Children imagine themselves in the role of President.

Strategies for Starting
Invite children to share their knowledge of the presidency. Discuss where the President lives and what the President does. Have a discussion about what it would be like if they were President and what they would do in that role. Encourage students to use the correct verb tense, "If I *were* President, I would . . ."

Introduce the Book
Display the book you made as a model. Ask what the title *If I Were President* means.

Make the Book
Duplicate and pass out pages 65–68 of this book. Either preassemble the books or help children assemble their books. You may want to brainstorm possible responses as a group to help children develop their ideas. Write students' ideas on the board for them to refer to as they make their books. Encourage children to draw pictures that support what they have written. Suggest that they draw themselves sitting behind the desk on the cover.

Share the Book
Invite students to share their books with partners or with the class. Ask them to respond to their peers' work with thoughtful questions or positive comments. You may want to model this with examples such as, "I like the way you said that if you were President you would make peace all over the world," or "How would you reach your goal of helping people get enough food?" Send the books home for students to read to family members and friends.

Beyond the Book
This book can be readily connected with Presidents' Day and a unit on the presidency. Make a bulletin board display featuring famous presidents such as Abraham Lincoln and George Washington, as well as the current president and recent presidents students recognize. Display students' books alongside the pictures.

TEACHING TIP: Use this book as a springboard to discuss other careers. Ask students to describe what they would do if they were astronauts, artists, teachers, or members of any other profession. You could also invite guests from the community to tell your class about their jobs.

Happy Valentine's Day

FEBRUARY   pages 69–74

Purpose
Children identify direct quotations. Children fill in talk balloons and learn about quotation marks.

Strategies for Starting
Discuss Valentine's Day. Ask:
Why do we celebrate Valentine's Day? Whom do you want to show love to on Valentine's Day? How can we show love to people every day?

Introduce the Book

Read aloud to the class the sample book that you made. You may want to use different voices for the characters so that students can hear the direct quotations. Ask students to guess what you wrote in the talk balloons. Then ask them how they figured this out. Invite students to predict the ending of the book.

Make the Book

Duplicate and pass out pages 69–74 of this book. Either preassemble the books or help children assemble their books. On page 2, invite children to draw a valentine and a rose. Ask students to find the direct quotations on each page by looking for the words inside quotation marks. Then have them copy the quotations into the talk balloons to reinforce the concept of using dialogue. Later, give children opportunities to add dialogue to their own writing.

Share the Book

Have children read their books aloud to the class. Ask children to act out the roles of frog, bunny, snail, minnow, and toad. Send the books home for children to read to family members and friends.

Beyond the Book

Invite children to make a valentine card for an animal of their choice. What message do they want to write to the animal? Do they love the stripes on a zebra or the way a cat purrs? Have children write and illustrate their cards, then add them to a Valentine's Day display along with the books they made.

How Big Is a Leprechaun?

MARCH   pages 75–79

Purpose

Children make size comparisons. Children review comparative adjectives to describe size relationships.

Strategies for Starting

Ask students to choose an object in the classroom. Then assign partners and have them use comparative adjectives to describe the size relationship between the two objects: *bigger, smaller, taller, shorter, wider,* and so on. For example, a student might say, "My pencil is taller than Sarah's eraser." Discuss leprechauns with the class. Ask: *Does anyone know what a leprechaun is? What do they look like? Do they bring good luck or bad luck? Are they real or imaginary?*

Introduce the Book

Share with the class the book you made as a model. Before you read each page aloud, you may want to ask students to describe the size relationship between the leprechaun and the object. Explain to students that on each page they will choose either "is" or "isn't" to complete each sentence. Review the use of contractions before students begin making their books.

Make the Book

Duplicate and pass out pages 75–79 of this book. Either preassemble the books or help children assemble their books. Have children determine the size relationship on each page and fill in either "is" or "isn't" on the line. On the last page, children can draw themselves either larger or smaller than the leprechaun.

Share the Book

Ask children to read their books aloud with partners, alternating pages. Then send the books home for children to share with family members and friends.

Beyond the Book

Have children use rulers to measure the length and width of various objects. Ask them to record their answers and then compare the sizes of various objects using comparative adjectives.

The Colors of the Earth

APRIL   pages 80–84

Purpose

Students recognize and celebrate the earth's beauty. Children review colors.

Strategies for Starting

Discuss the many beautiful components of the earth: oceans, grass, trees, sand, flowers, rainbows, animals, people, and even the sun, moon, and sky. Have children consider these elements and describe them using color words. Invite students to think about why we call the earth our home. Ask: *What is a home? Is the earth a home? What makes it a home and who lives in it?*

Introduce the Book

Read aloud to the class the model book you made. Let children suggest colors to fill in the blanks. Point out the pattern of the text and the connections between the illustrations and the words.

Make the Book

Duplicate and pass out pages 80–84 of this book. Either preassemble the books or help children assemble their books. Read through the book together. Invite children to illustrate the pages to correspond to the text. On page 1, have children color each object and then write the color on the line. On pages 2–7, ask children to write the name of an appropriate color on the line. On each page, students can add a picture of themselves or other people enjoying nature.

Share the Book

Read the book aloud together. Send the books home for children to share with family members. After they have returned the books, have children add *The Colors of the Earth* to their personal libraries.

Beyond the Book

- Connect this book with the study of Earth Day (April 22). Discuss how we can care for the earth by picking up litter, recycling, saving energy, planting trees, saving water, avoiding pollution, and caring for wildlife. Engage the class in an environmental project, such as setting up a recycling station in your classroom.

- Have children write letters to their parents to remind them of what they can do to care for the environment. Develop a checklist of things that children and their families can do to help care for the earth. Make copies and send them home with children's letters.

TEACHING TIP: Read books and stories about caring for the earth and appreciating its beauty. Make a class mural showing ways we can protect the environment. Display it in the hallway with written explanations of what students have depicted.

It's Springtime!

MAY   pages 85–88

Purpose
Children develop expressive language and vocabulary about spring. Children fill in -*ing* verbs. Children identify the signs of spring.

Strategies for Starting
Have children share their observations of spring. Encourage them to express their ideas using the same pattern as the book, such as "The robins are singing" or "The worms are crawling."

Introduce the Book
Read aloud the sample book that you made. Emphasize the -*ing* verbs. Remind children that the illustrations provide clues to the text.

Make the Book
Duplicate and pass out pages 85–88 of this book. Either preassemble the books or help children assemble their books. As a group, brainstorm a list of possible -*ing* verbs for children to use as they make their books.

Share the Book
Invite children to share their books with partners. Encourage children to write positive comments on the back covers of one another's books. Have them take the books home to read to their families and then bring the books back with responses.

Beyond the Book
Make a bulletin board with the many signs of spring mentioned in the book. Encourage students to watch for signs of spring and record on the bulletin board where and when they take place. Investigate and record the time the sun rises and sets each day, as well as the daily high and low temperature. Challenge students to fill in a bar graph based on this information and then make predictions about tomorrow's weather.

My Memory Book

JUNE   pages 89–93

Purpose
Children reflect upon the school year. Children write about special activities and people that shaped the year. Children write about what they learned and enjoyed.

Strategies for Starting
Invite reflection and discussion about the school year. Ask: *Do you remember the first day of the school year? What was it like? How did you feel? What things have you learned since then? What activities have you enjoyed? What people helped to make this a special year? What were the most memorable events of the year? Why?*

Introduce the Book
Read aloud the sample book that you made. Use it as a springboard for further discussion. Encourage students to think of their own favorite memories.

Make the Book

Duplicate and pass out pages 89–93 of this book. Either preassemble the books or help children assemble the books. As children are making their books, ask them questions to help them develop thoughtful, personal recollections. On the cover, invite children to draw people, places, or things that they will remember from the year. Encourage children to draw illustrations that support their writing. The back cover, titled "Autographs," is a place for children to sign one another's books.

Share the Book

Have students sit in a circle and pass their books around for others to read and then sign. You may want to invite the people students wrote about in their books, such as administrators, support staff, gym teachers, and art teachers. They will be glad to know that students included them in their memory books. Students will also enjoy asking the guests to sign their books.

Beyond the Book

Invite students to choose one memory from their book—either a person, a special event, or something they learned. Ask them to write more about it and then to paint or draw a large illustration to support what they have written. You can hang these pieces along with the books on a bulletin board display titled "Looking Back on _____ Grade."

TEACHING TIP: This memory book is a wonderful way to reflect on and bring closure to the school year. Encourage children to save their memory books as well as all of their Write & Read Books. Emphasize how special it will be for children to look at these books in the future and remember what it was like to be their age.

_____
date

Dear Family,

As part of our literacy program, our class is making Write & Read Books. The stories in these books follow simple patterns that we practice reading in class. The children are very proud of these books and want to share them with you. Please try to set aside time to read and talk about the books together.

On the back of each book you will find a page labeled "Comments." It will mean a lot to your child if you write one or two **positive** comments about the book or the way your child reads it. For example, you might remark on the story, the ideas, the illustrations, the handwriting, or the overall presentation. You might also comment on the way your child reads with expression or fluency, figures out hard words, uses context clues, is increasing sight vocabulary, or has improved in general.

Please return the books with your comments back to school by

_____.

Many thanks for your participation. Your interest and support will mean a lot to your young reader.

Sincerely,

_____

School Bells Ring

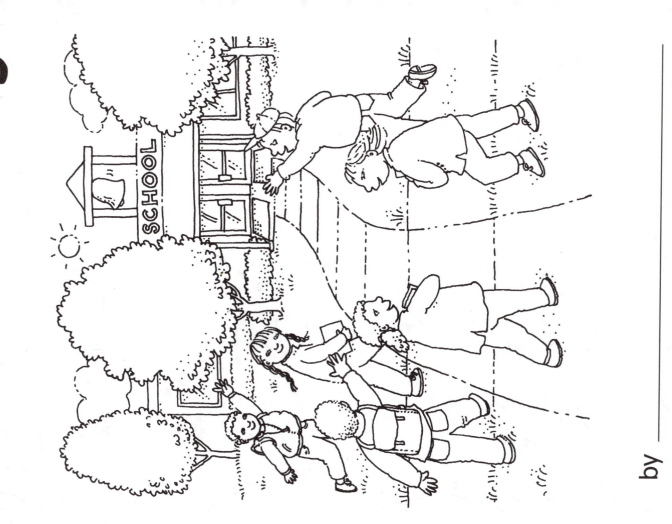

by _____

Month-by-Month Write & Read Books Scholastic Professional Books

Comments

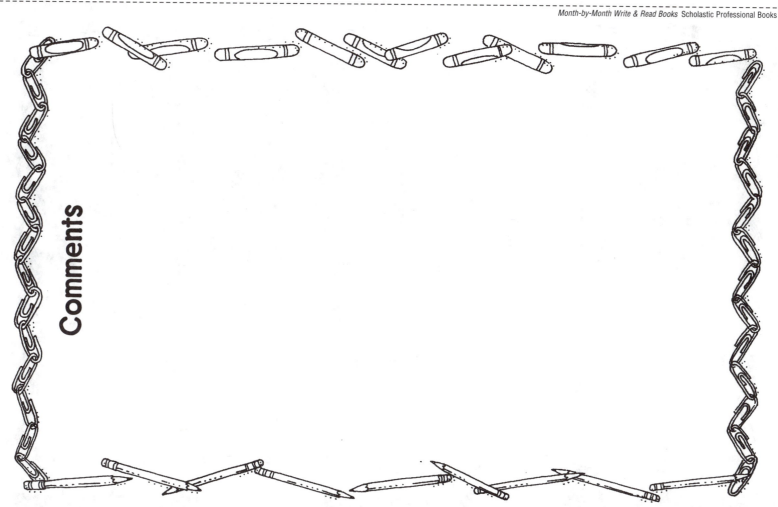

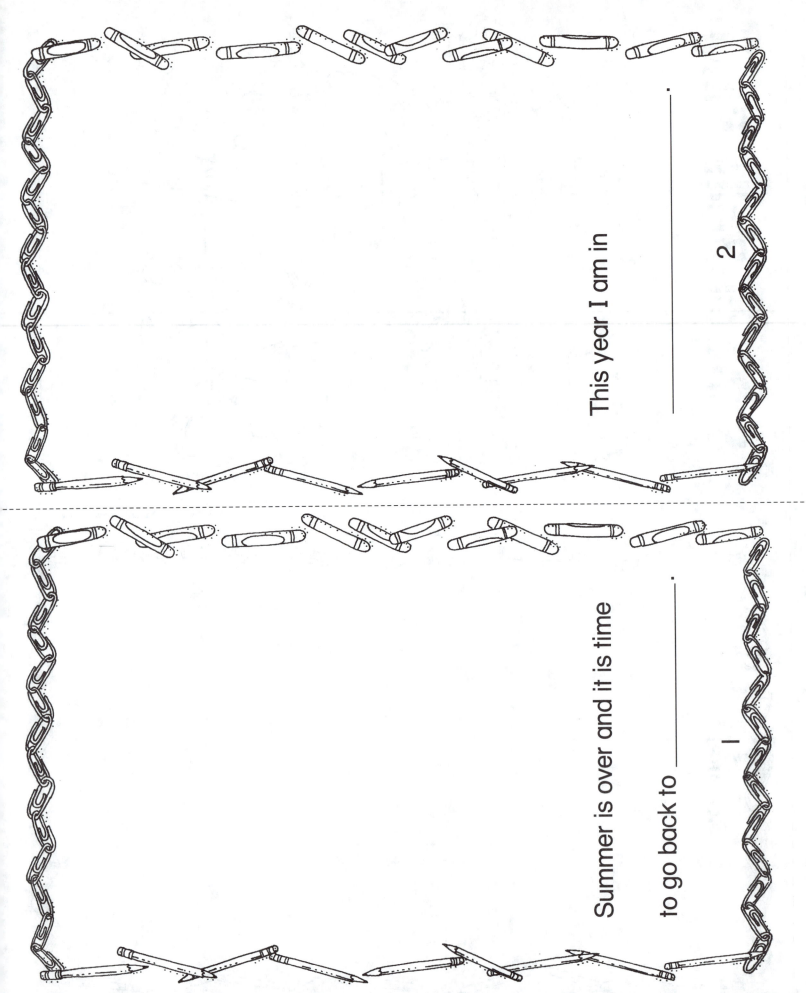

This year I am in

_____.

2

Summer is over and it is time

to go back to _____

I

My favorite part of school is

_____ .

4

In school we learn to

_____ and

_____ .

3

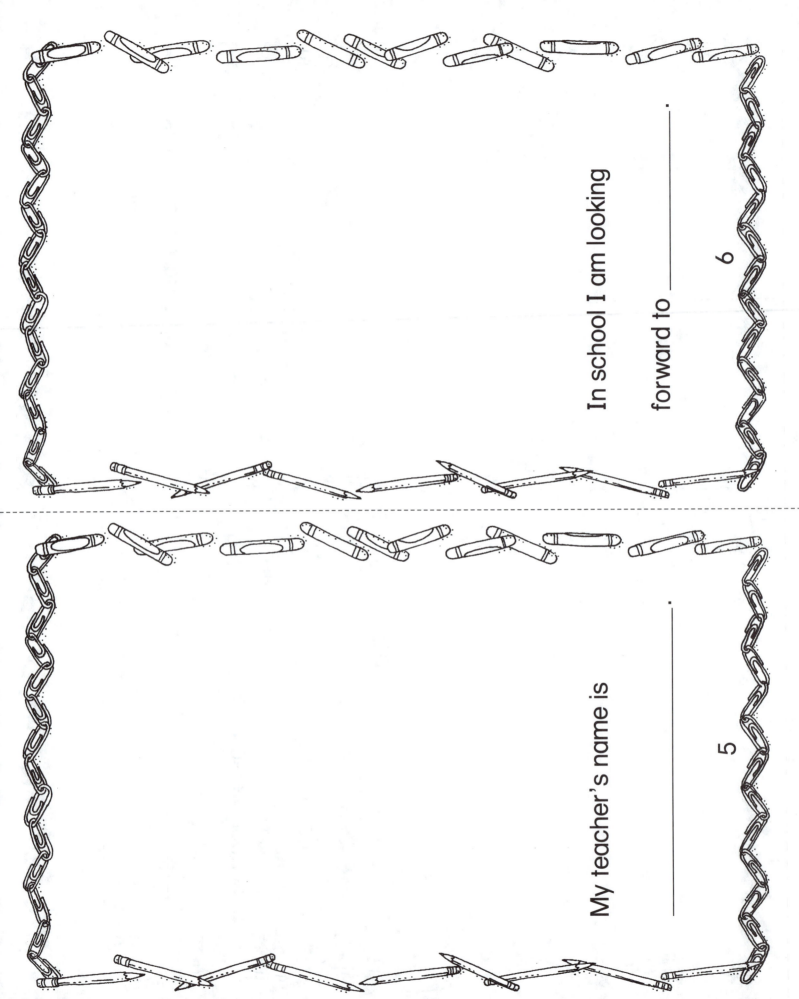

In school I am looking

forward to _____ .

6

My teacher's name is

_____ .

5

Autumn

by _____

Month-by-Month Write & Read Books Scholastic Professional Books

Comments

23

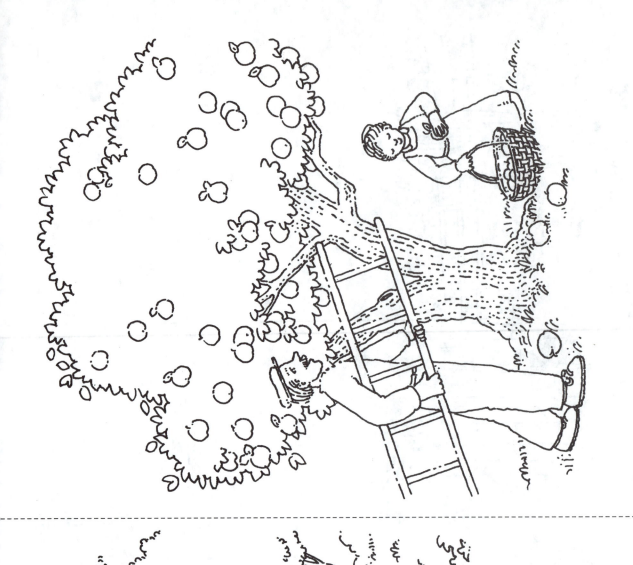

I see _____
in the trees, ready to be picked.

2

Autumn is here and I see
changes all around me.

I see colorful _____
falling from trees.

1

I see _____
storing acorns for the winter.

4

I see _____
growing fatter in the fields.

3

I see all of these changes in the fall. My favorite part of autumn is _____

6

At night, I see the _____ get dark earlier.

5

Fall Harvest

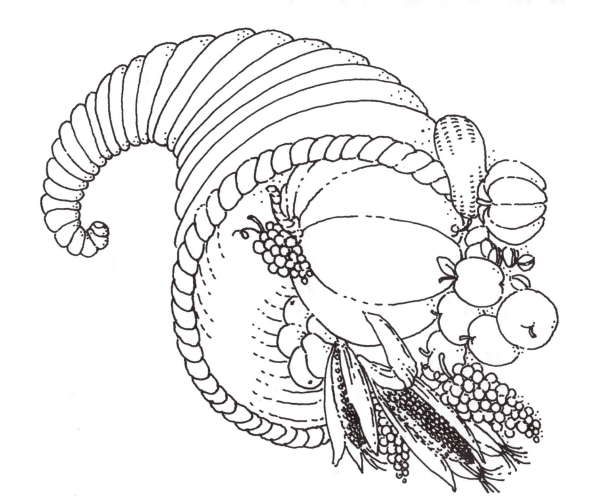

by _____

Month-by-Month Write & Read Books Scholastic Professional Books

Comments

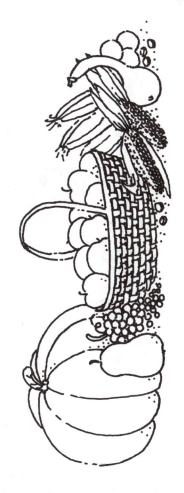

Pumpkins in the patch,
Pumpkins in the patch,
Pick, pick,
Pick, pick,

Pumpkins _____ _____ _____.

2

Apples in the orchard,
Apples in the orchard,
Ripen, ripen,
Ripen, ripen,

Apples _____ _____ _____.

1

Wheat in the field,
Wheat in the field,
Reap, reap,
Reap, reap,

Wheat _____ _____ .

4

Carrots in the ground,
Carrots in the ground,
Dig, dig,
Dig, dig,

Carrots _____ _____ .

3

Food in the market,
Food in the market,
Yum, yum,
Yum, yum,

Food _____ .

6

Vegetables in the garden,
Vegetables in the garden,
Harvest, harvest,
Harvest, harvest,

Vegetables _____ .

5

Apples, Apples, Apples

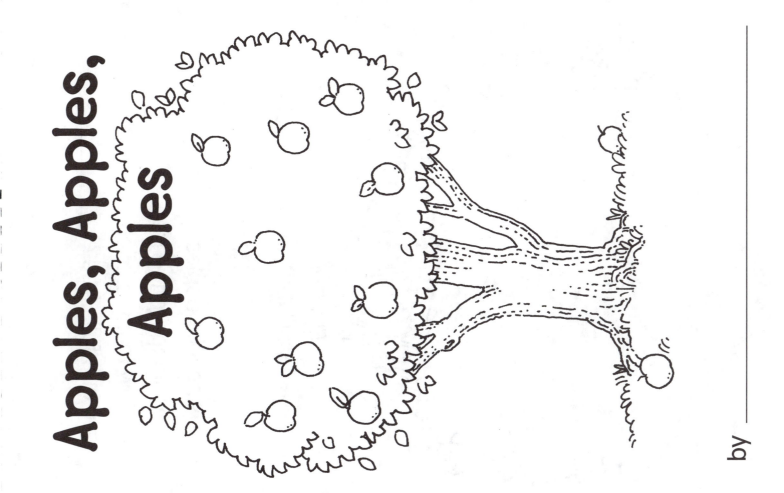

by _____

Comments

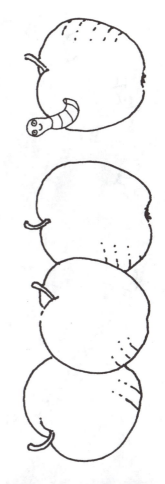

Nine little apples
hanging from a tree.
How many are left
if one falls free? ____

2

Ten little apples
hanging from a tree.
How many are left
if one falls free? ____

1

Seven little apples
hanging from a tree.
How many are left
if one falls free? _____

4

Eight little apples
hanging from a tree.
How many are left
if one falls free? _____

3

Five little apples
hanging from a tree.
How many are left
if one falls free? _____

6

Six little apples
hanging from a tree.
How many are left
if one falls free? _____

5

Three little apples
hanging from a tree.
How many are left
if one falls free? _____

8

Four little apples
hanging from a tree.
How many are left
if one falls free? _____

7

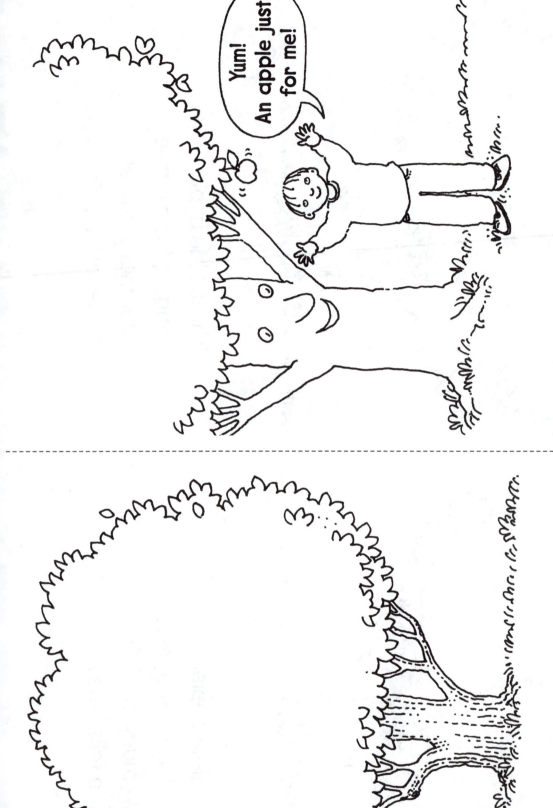

One little apple
hanging from a tree.
How many are left
if it falls free? _____

10

Two little apples
hanging from a tree.
How many are left
if one falls free? _____

9

Tiny Spider

by _____

Month-by-Month Write & Read Books Scholastic Professional Books

Comments

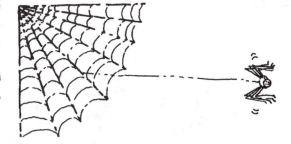

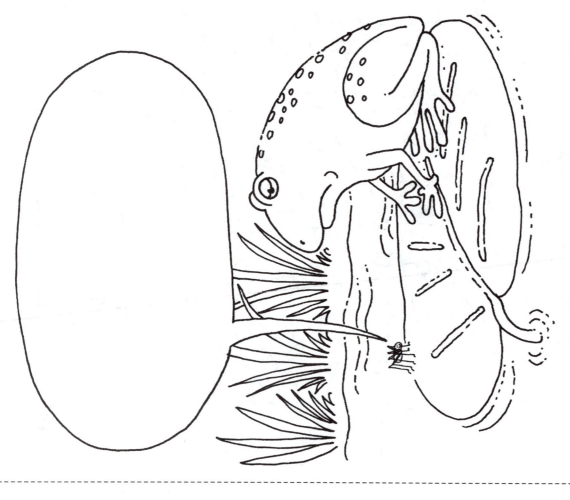

First he met a frowning frog,
sitting on a lily pad.
"Hello there, frog," the tiny
spider said.

2

A tiny spider was lonely
in his web.
"Who can I meet
today?" he wondered.

1

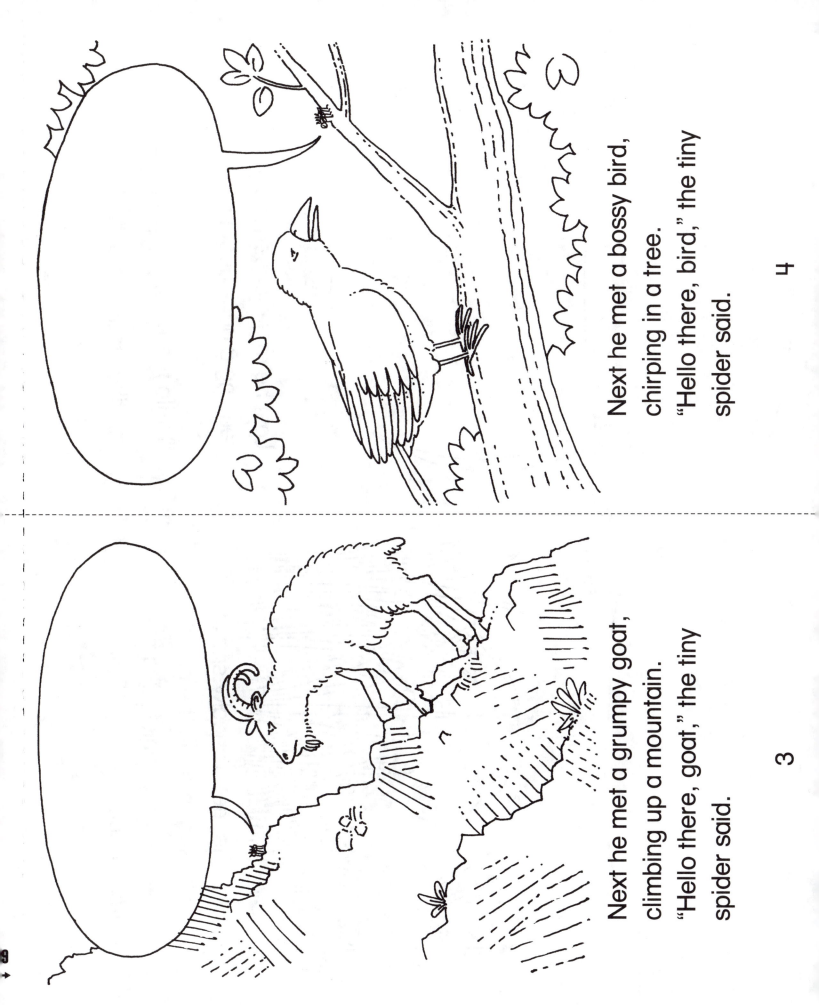

Next he met a bossy bird,
chirping in a tree.
"Hello there, bird," the tiny
spider said.

4

Next he met a grumpy goat,
climbing up a mountain.
"Hello there, goat," the tiny
spider said.

3

Last he met a cheerful child,
reading a book about a spider.

"Hello there, ___YOUR NAME HERE___,"
the tiny spider said. "Let's go play!"

6

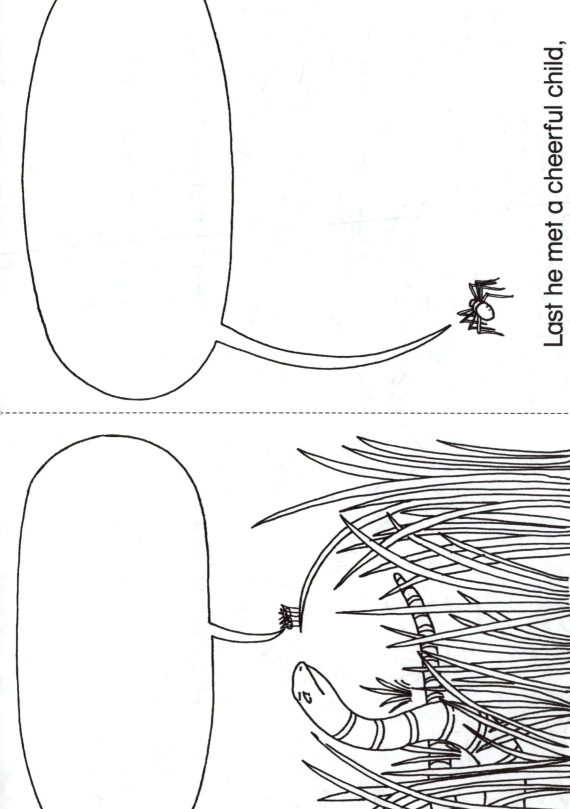

Next he met a sneaky snake,
slithering through the grass.
"Hello there, snake," the tiny
spider said.

5

I Am Thankful

by _____

Comments

I am thankful for the _____ that I eat.

2

I am thankful for many things.

1

I am thankful for the

_____ that I live in.

4

I am thankful for the

_____ that I wear.

3

Month-by-Month Write & Read Books Scholastic Professional Books

I am thankful for the

_____
that I love.

6

I am thankful for the

_____
that I play with.

5

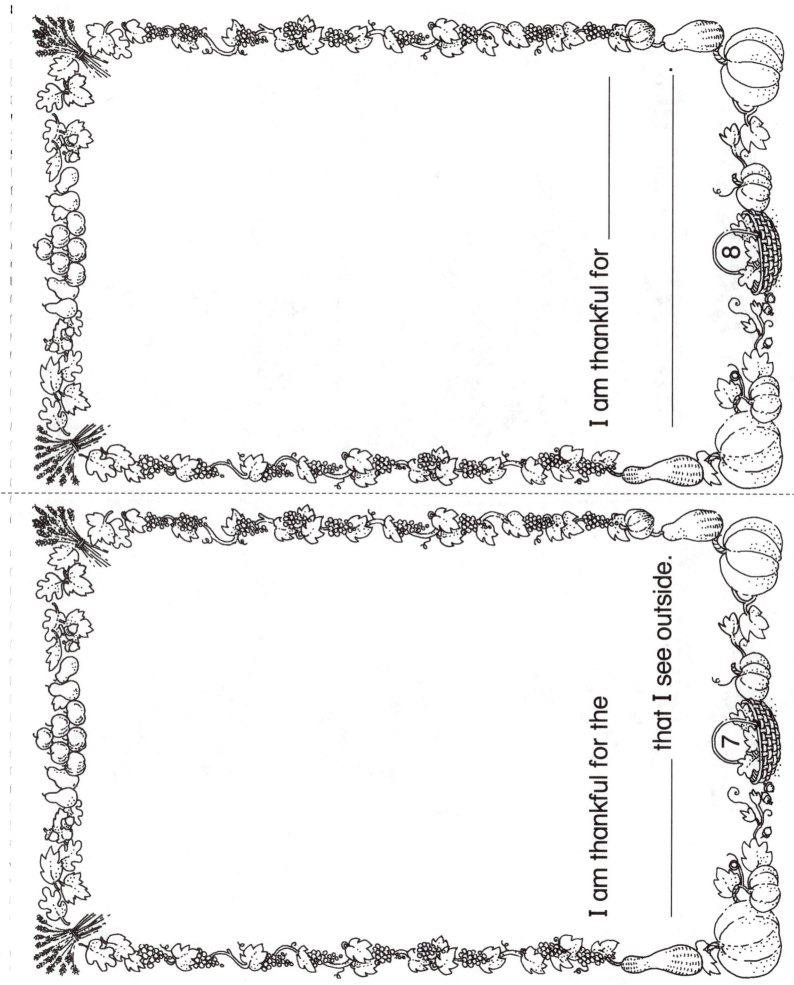

I am thankful for the _____
_____ that I see outside.

7

I am thankful for _____
_____.

8

One Cold, Snowy Morning

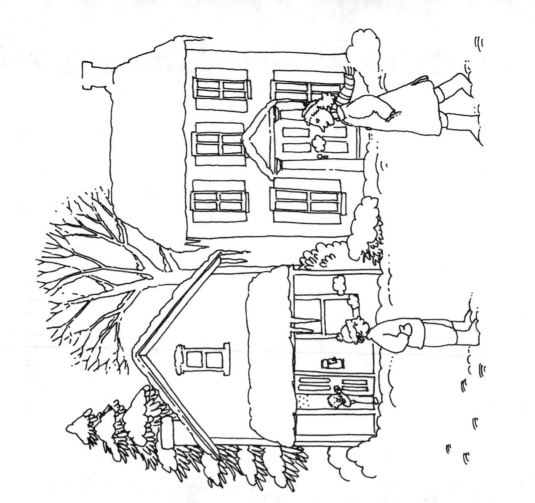

by _____

Month-by-Month Write & Read Books Scholastic Professional Books

Comments

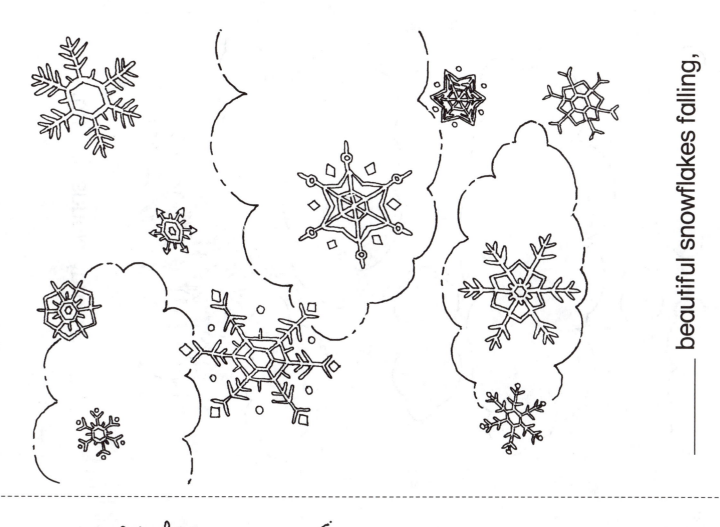

_____ beautiful snowflakes falling,

2

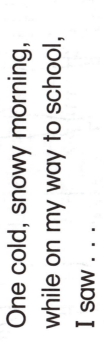

One cold, snowy morning,
while on my way to school,
I saw . . . .

1

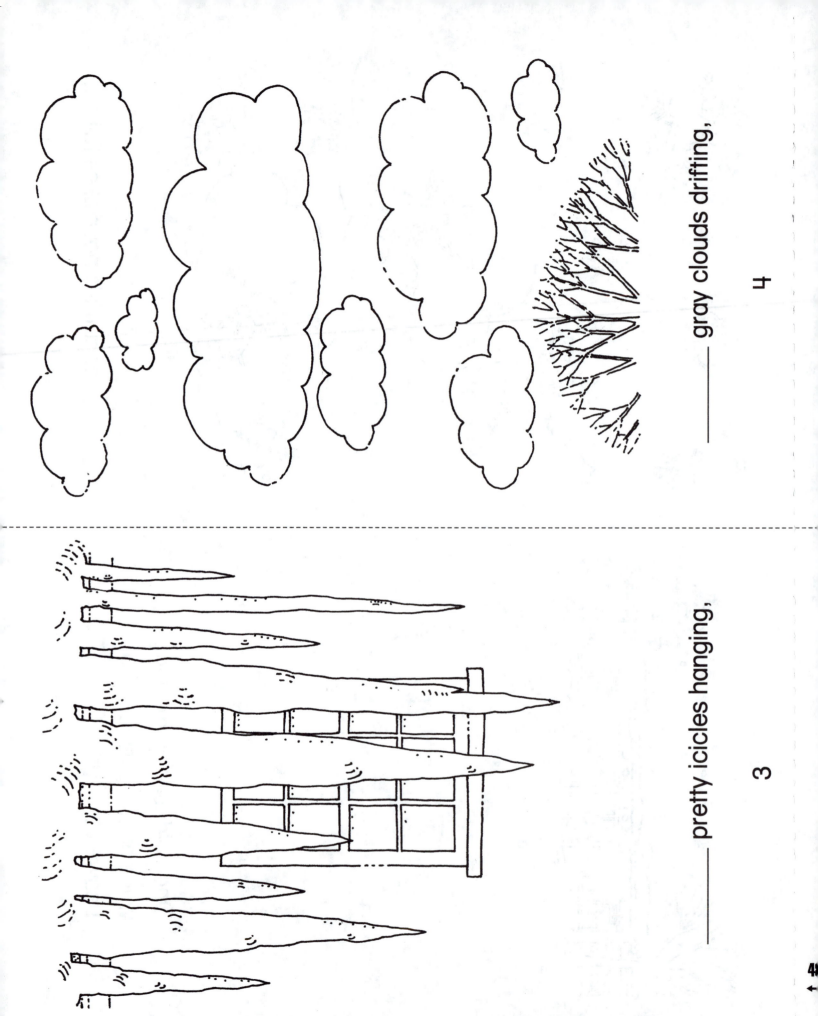

——— gray clouds drifting,

4

——— pretty icicles hanging,

3

Month-by-Month Write & Read Books Scholastic Professional Books

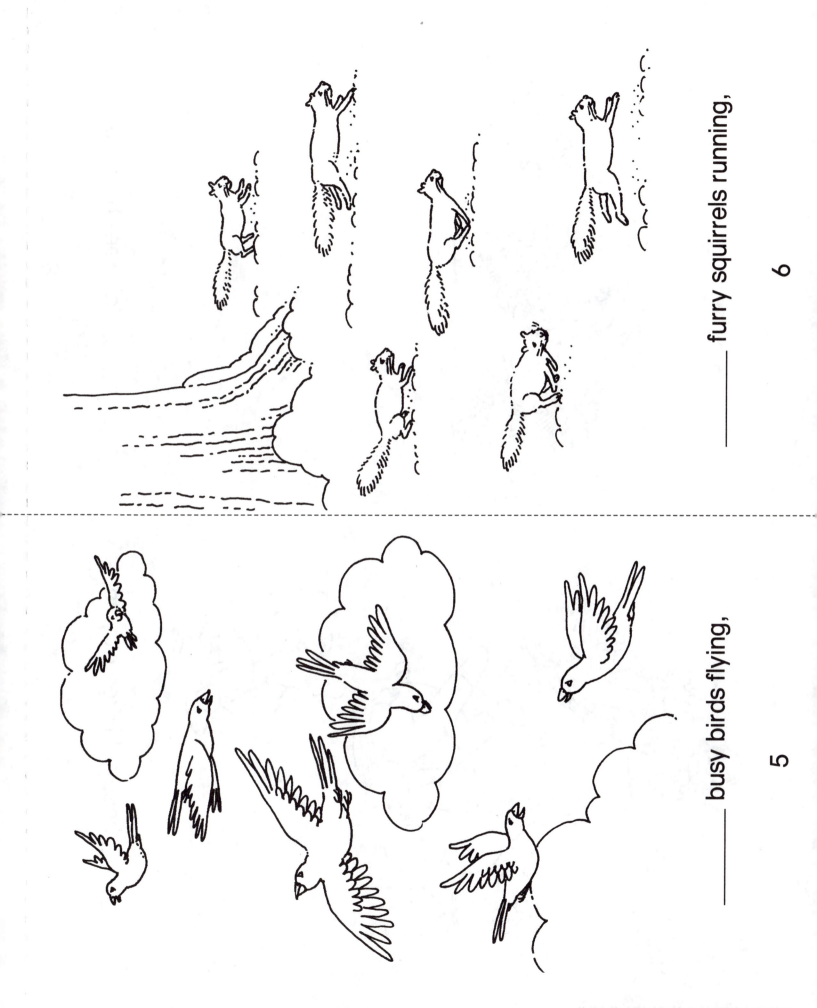

—— furry squirrels running,

6

—— busy birds flying,

5

——— tall trees bending,

8

——— happy children playing,

7

—— big plows plowing,

10

—— snow shovels shoveling,

9

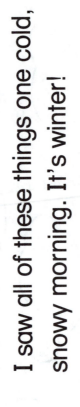

I saw all of these things one cold, snowy morning. It's winter!

12

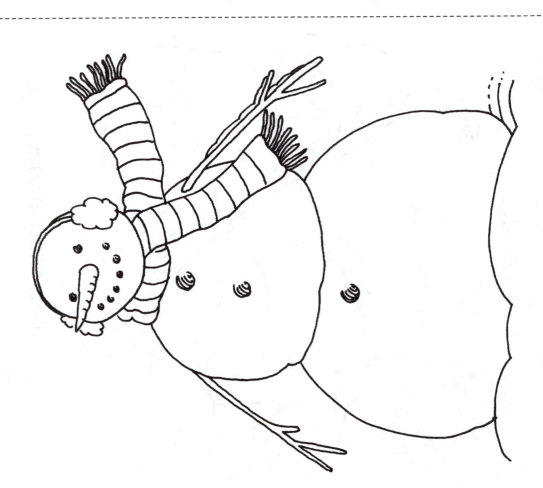

and ———— snowman smiling!

11

How to Make a Snowman

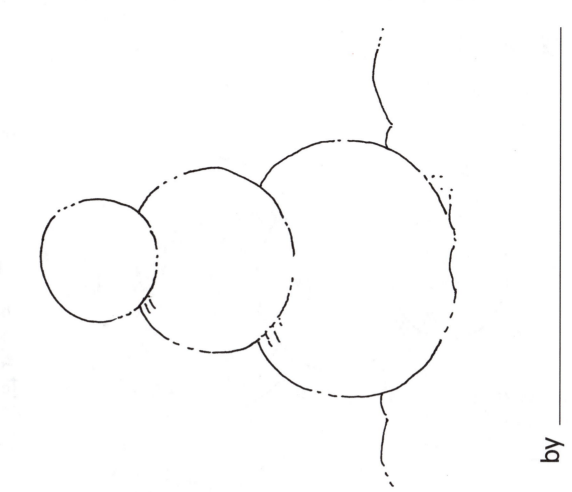

by _____

Month-by-Month Write & Read Books Scholastic Professional Books

Comments

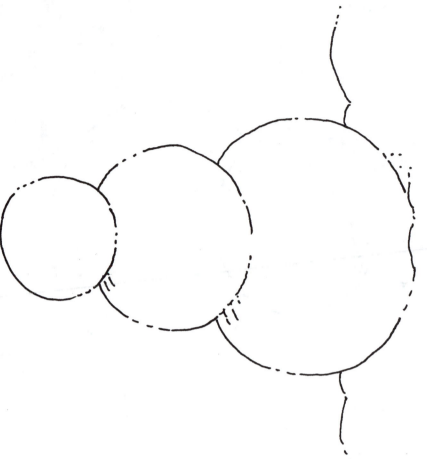

First I rolled ⎯⎯⎯ balls
of snow.
I stacked them on top of
each other.

2

This is how I made my snowman.

1

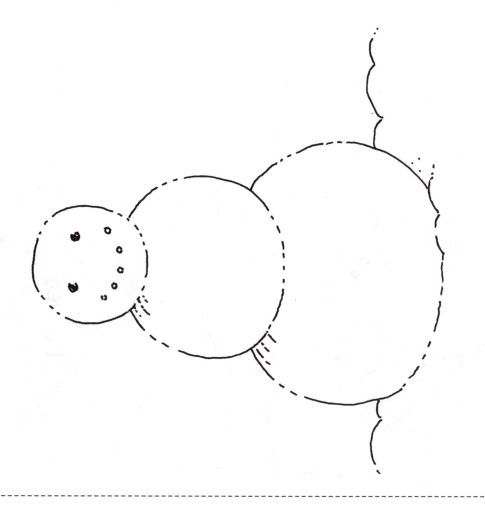

Then, I added _____ coal eyes.

3

Then, I added _____ gumdrops
for the mouth.

4

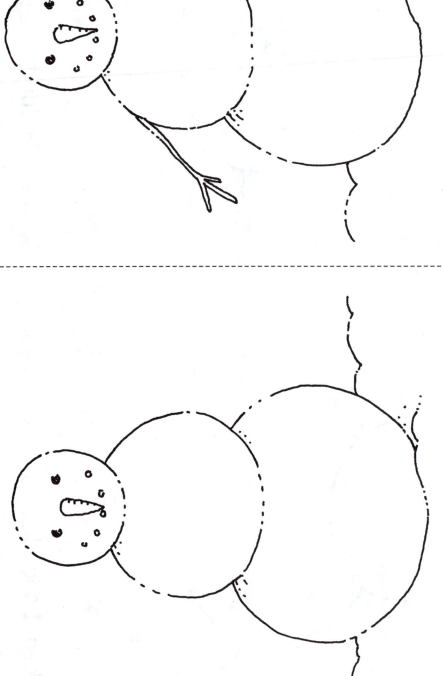

Then, I added _____ branches for the arms.

6

Then, I added _____ carrot for the nose.

5

At last, I dressed him in a scarf and hat.
I named my snowman _____.

8

Then, I added _____ pebbles
for the buttons on his tummy.

7

100 Is Fun to Count

by _____

Month-by-Month Write & Read Books Scholastic Professional Books

1 2 3 4 5 6 7 8 9 10 11 12 13 14 15 16 17 18 19 **20** 21 22 23 24 25 26 27 28 29 **30** 31 32 33 34 35 36 37 38 39 **40** 41 42 43 44 45 46 47 48 49 **50** 51 52 53 54 55 56 57 58 59 **60** 61 62 63 64 65 66 67 68 69 **70** 71 72 73 74 75 76 77 78 79 **80** 81 82 83 84 85 86 87 88 89 **90** 91 92 93 94 95 96 97 98 99 **100**

Comments

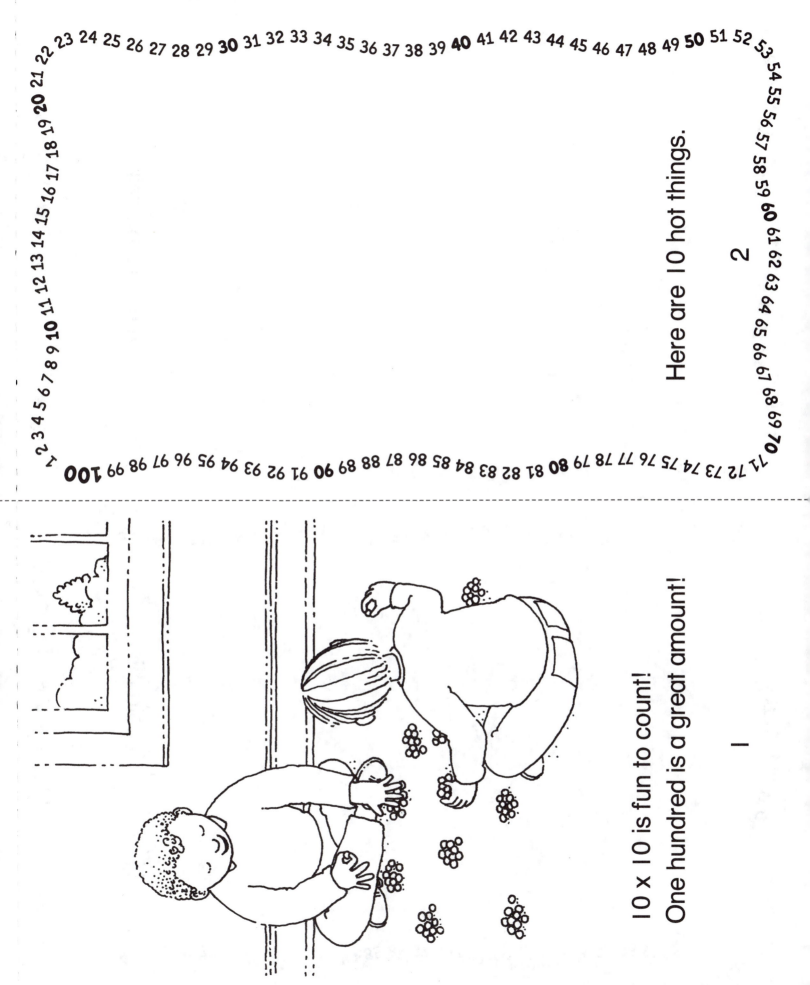

Here are 10 hot things.

2

10 x 10 is fun to count!
One hundred is a great amount!

1

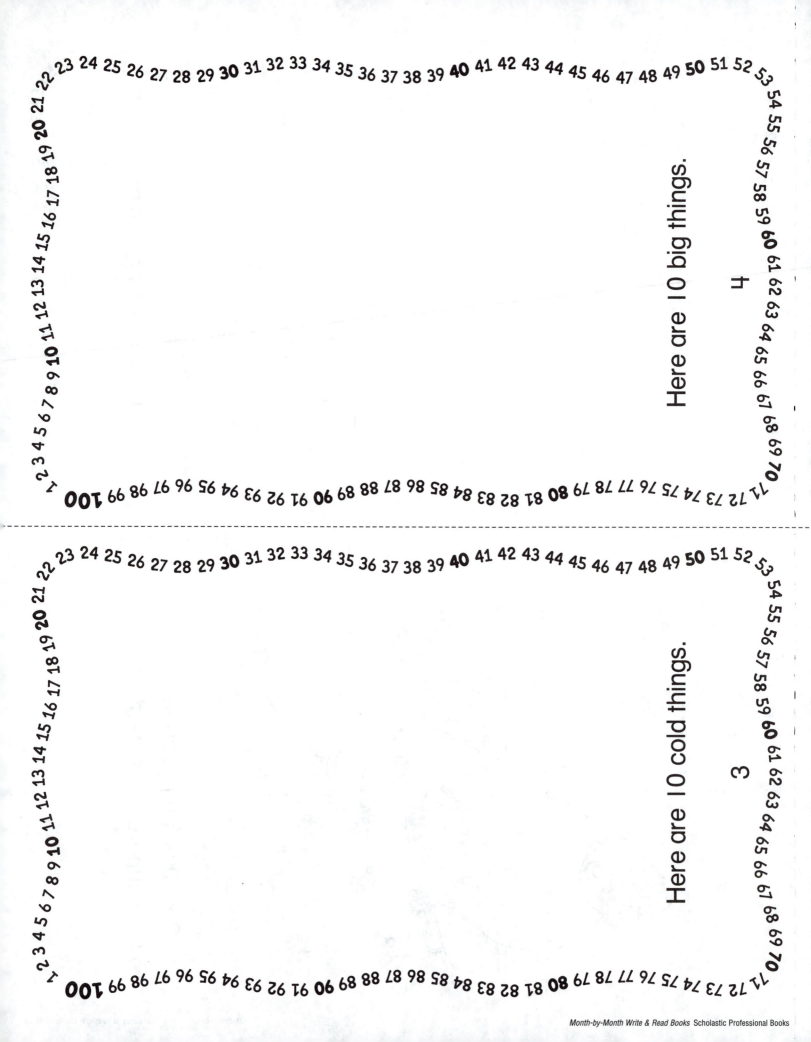

1 2 3 4 5 6 7 8 9 **10** 11 12 13 14 15 16 17 18 19 **20** 21 22 23 24 25 26 27 28 29 **30** 31 32 33 34 35 36 37 38 39 **40** 41 42 43 44 45 46 47 48 49 **50** 51 52 53 54 55 56 57 58 59 **60** 61 62 63 64 65 66 67 68 69 **70** 71 72 73 74 75 76 77 78 79 **80** 81 82 83 84 85 86 87 88 89 **90** 91 92 93 94 95 96 97 98 99 **100**

4

Here are 10 big things.

1 2 3 4 5 6 7 8 9 **10** 11 12 13 14 15 16 17 18 19 **20** 21 22 23 24 25 26 27 28 29 **30** 31 32 33 34 35 36 37 38 39 **40** 41 42 43 44 45 46 47 48 49 **50** 51 52 53 54 55 56 57 58 59 **60** 61 62 63 64 65 66 67 68 69 **70** 71 72 73 74 75 76 77 78 79 **80** 81 82 83 84 85 86 87 88 89 **90** 91 92 93 94 95 96 97 98 99 **100**

3

Here are 10 cold things.

Top half

Border numbers: 1 2 3 4 5 6 7 8 9 10 11 12 13 14 15 16 17 18 19 20 21 22 23 24 25 26 27 28 29 30 31 32 33 34 35 36 37 38 39 40 41 42 43 44 45 46 47 48 49 50 51 52 53 54 55 56 57 58 59 60 61 62 63 64 65 66 67 68 69 70 71 72 73 74 75 76 77 78 79 80 81 82 83 84 85 86 87 88 89 90 91 92 93 94 95 96 97 98 99 100

Here are 10 round things.

6

Bottom half

Border numbers: 1 2 3 4 5 6 7 8 9 10 11 12 13 14 15 16 17 18 19 20 21 22 23 24 25 26 27 28 29 30 31 32 33 34 35 36 37 38 39 40 41 42 43 44 45 46 47 48 49 50 51 52 53 54 55 56 57 58 59 60 61 62 63 64 65 66 67 68 69 70 71 72 73 74 75 76 77 78 79 80 81 82 83 84 85 86 87 88 89 90 91 92 93 94 95 96 97 98 99 100

Here are 10 small things.

5

Month-by-Month Write & Read Books Scholastic Professional Books

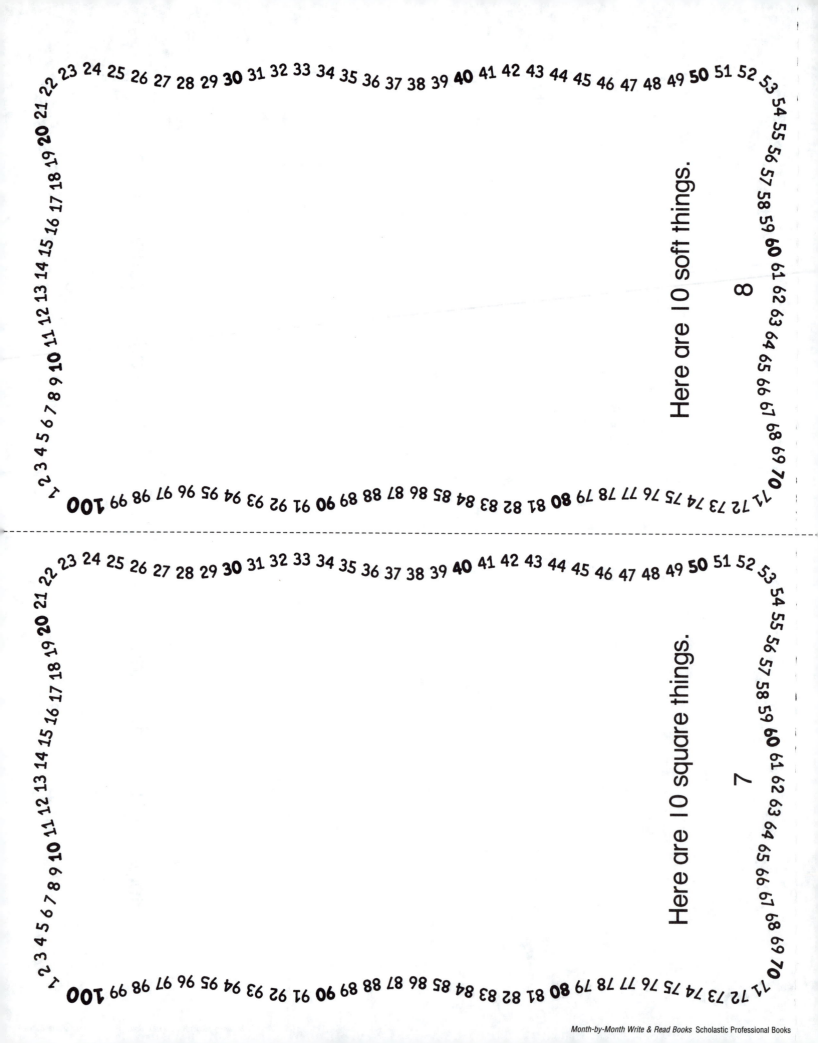

Here are 10 soft things.

8

Here are 10 square things.

7

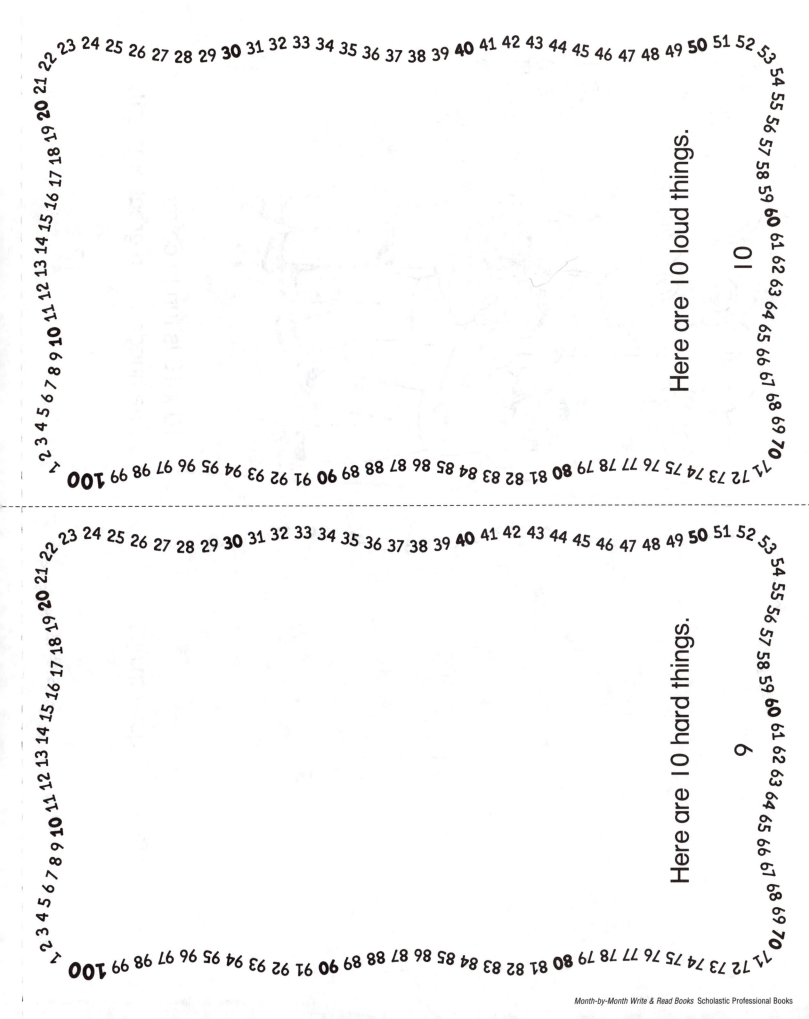

Here are 10 loud things.

10

Here are 10 hard things.

9

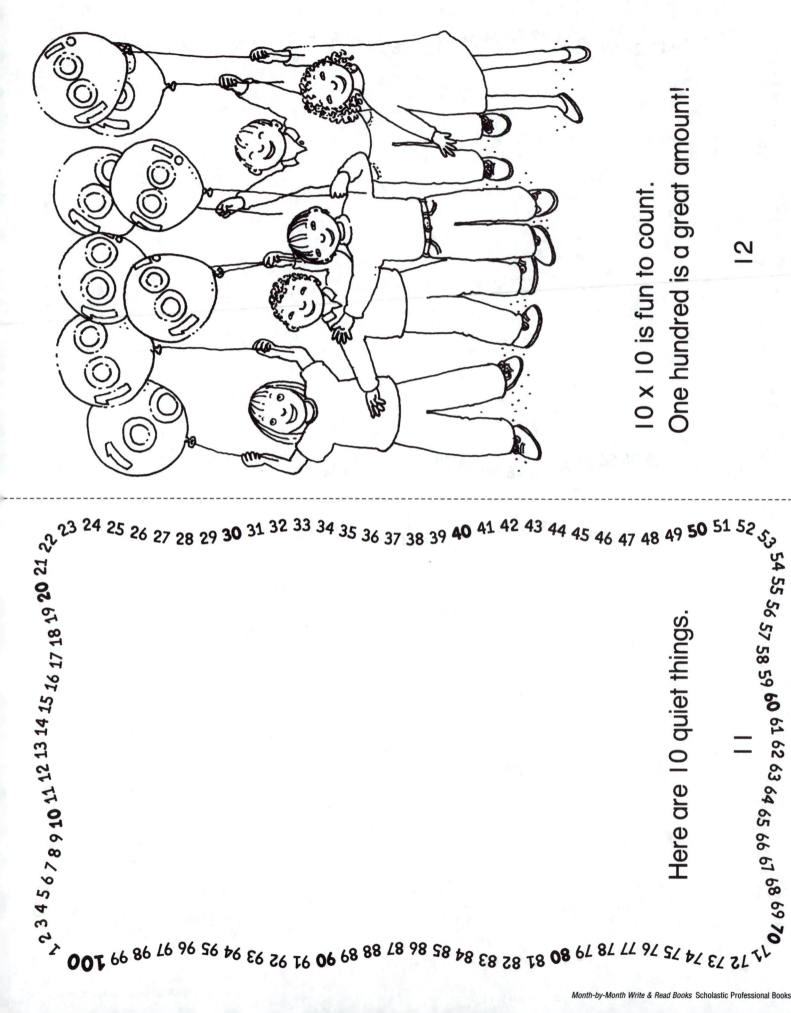

10 x 10 is fun to count.
One hundred is a great amount!

12

Here are 10 quiet things.

11

1 2 3 4 5 6 7 8 9 10 11 12 13 14 15 16 17 18 19 20 21 22 23 24 25 26 27 28 29 30 31 32 33 34 35 36 37 38 39 40 41 42 43 44 45 46 47 48 49 50 51 52 53 54 55 56 57 58 59 60 61 62 63 64 65 66 67 68 69 70 71 72 73 74 75 76 77 78 79 80 81 82 83 84 85 86 87 88 89 90 91 92 93 94 95 96 97 98 99 100

If I Were President

by _____

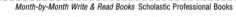

Comments

If I were President, I would eat

_____.

2

If I were President, the first thing

I would do is _____

_____.

1

If I were President, I would have

a pet _____

named _____.

4

If I were President, I would travel

to _____.

3

If I were President, I would help

_____.

6

If I were President, I would pass

a law that _____.

5

Happy Valentine's Day

by _____

Comments

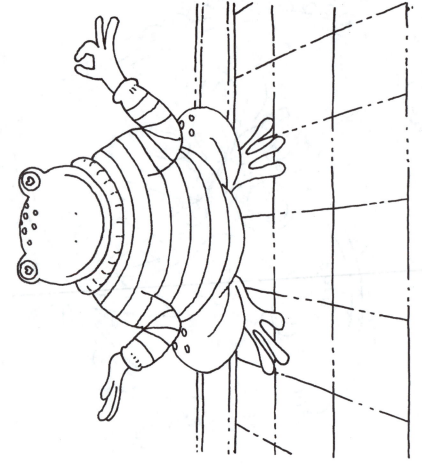

He made a fancy red card
and picked a pretty red rose.
Who would he give them to
on Valentine's Day?

2

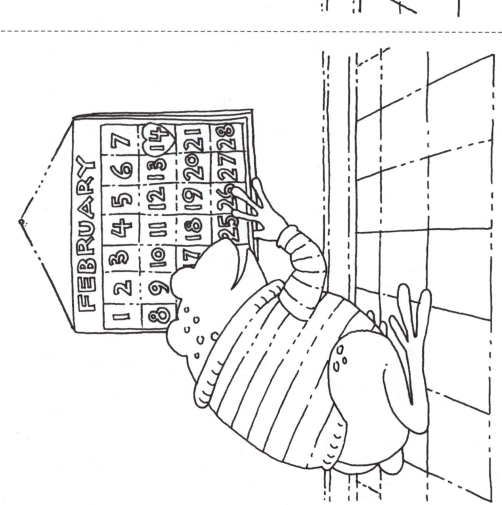

There once was a frog with
a very big heart.
Who would be his valentine
on Valentine's Day?

1

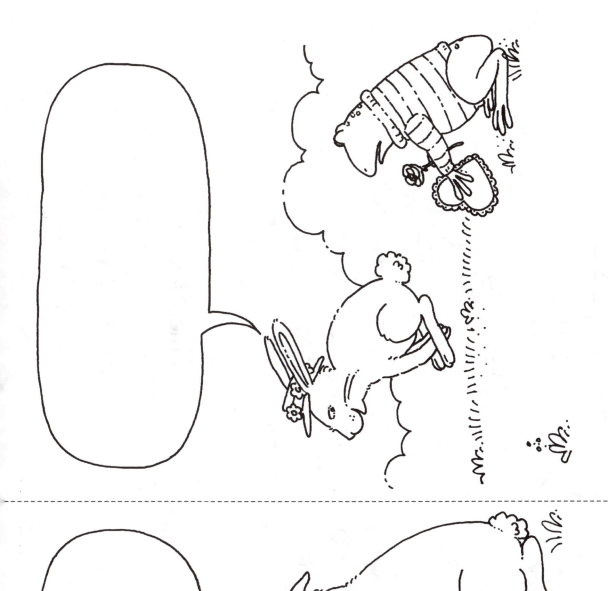

Just then Betty Bunny hopped by.
"Will you be my valentine?"
he asked.

3

"Not me," said Betty Bunny.
"My valentine is a squirrel."
And she hopped away.

4

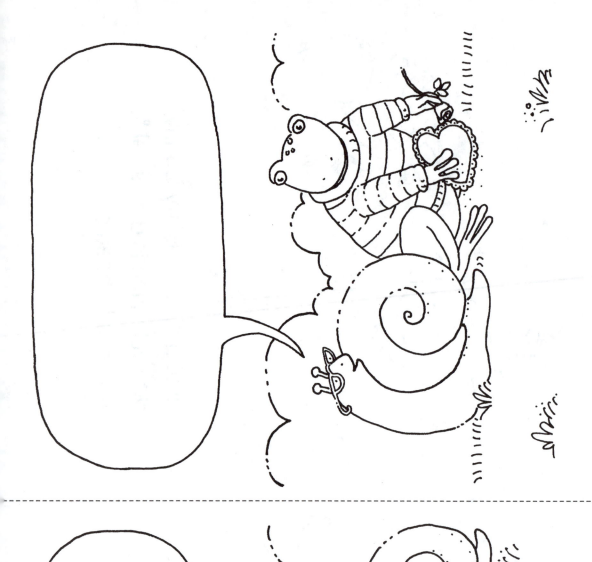

"Not me," said Sally Snail.
"My valentine is a spider."
And she crawled away.

6

Just then Sally Snail crawled by.
"Will you be my valentine?"
he asked.

5

"Not me," said Molly Minnow.
"My valentine is a turtle."
And she swam away.

8

Just then Molly Minnow swam by.
"Will you be my valentine?"
he asked.

7

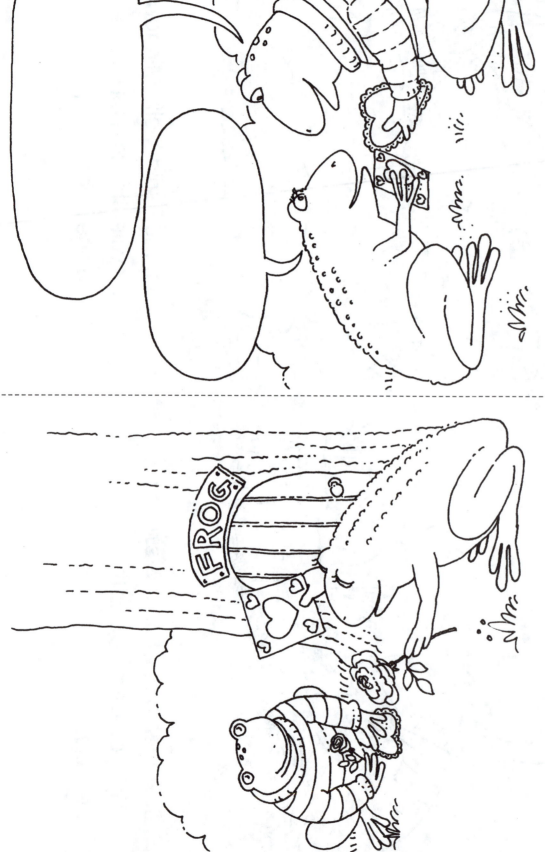

"Will you be my valentine?"
she asked.
"Of course!" said the frog.
"Happy Valentine's Day!"

10

The frog hopped home, and
at his door was Tammy Toad.
She held a red rose and a
fancy red card.

9

How Big Is a Leprechaun?

by _____

Month-by-Month Write & Read Books Scholastic Professional Books

Comments

A leprechaun _____ bigger than an apple.

is / isn't

2

How big do you think a leprechaun is?

1

A leprechaun _____ is / isn't _____ taller than a lamppost.

4

A leprechaun _____ is / isn't _____ bigger than a whale.

3

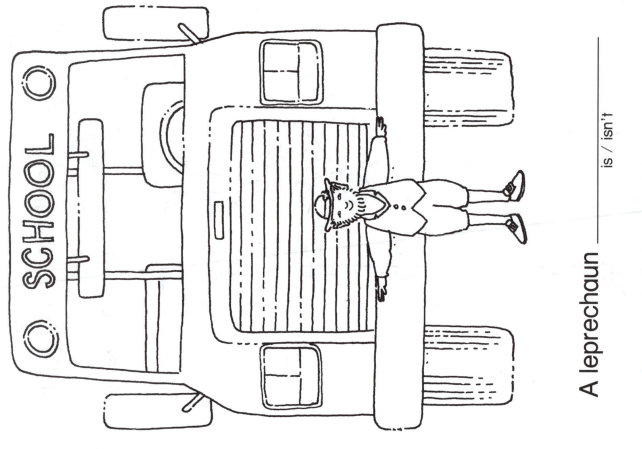

A leprechaun _____ is / isn't

wider than a school bus.

6

A leprechaun _____ is / isn't

taller than a nail.

5

A leprechaun _____ wider than a snail.
is / isn't

7

A leprechaun _____ larger than me.
is / isn't

Look at the picture and you'll see!

8

The Colors of the Earth

by _____

Month-by-Month Write & Read Books Scholastic Professional Books

Comments

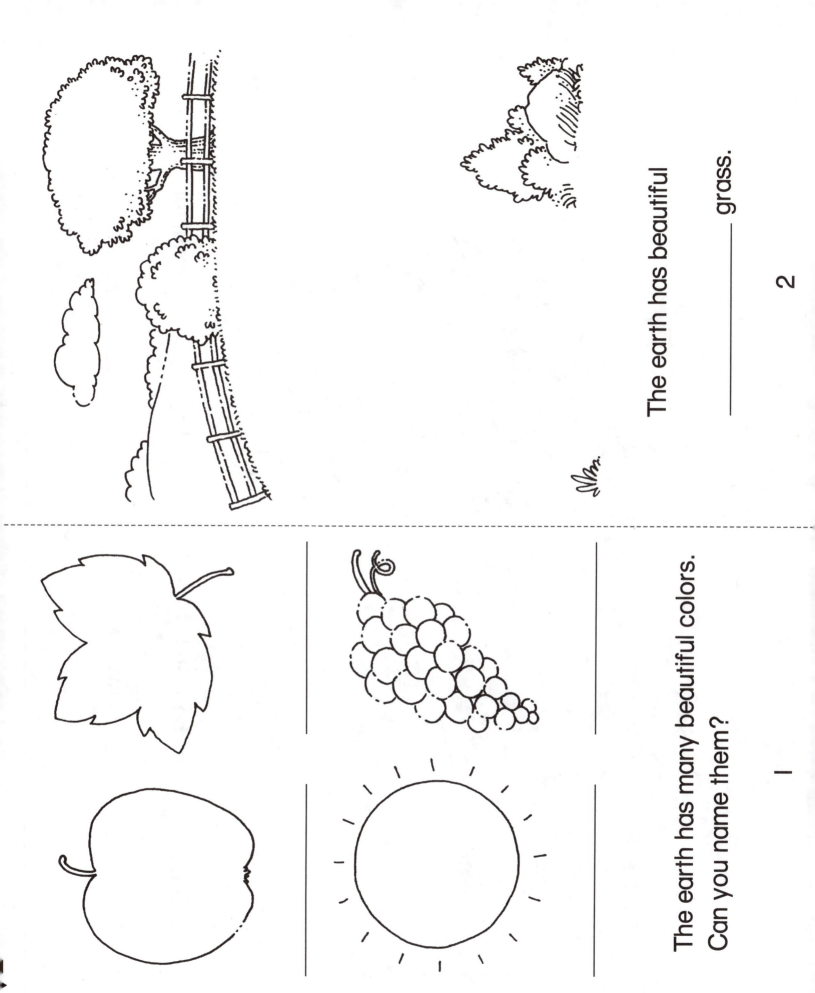

The earth has beautiful

_____
grass.

2

The earth has many beautiful colors.
Can you name them?

1

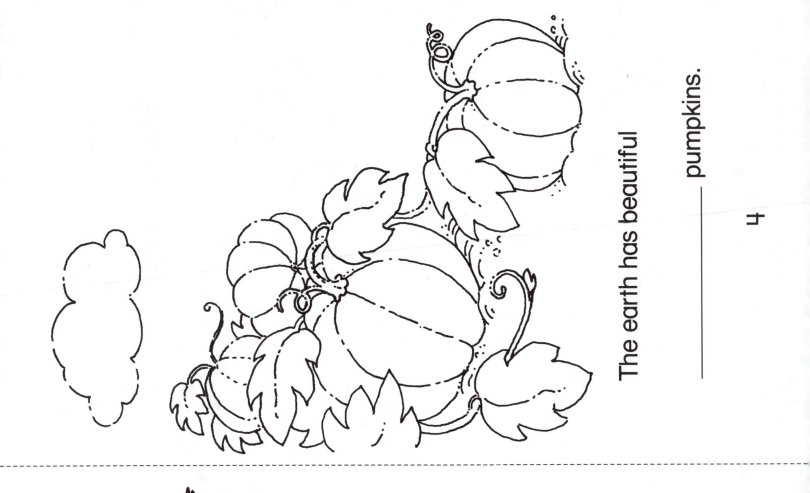

The earth has beautiful

—— pumpkins.

4

The earth has a beautiful

—— sky.

3

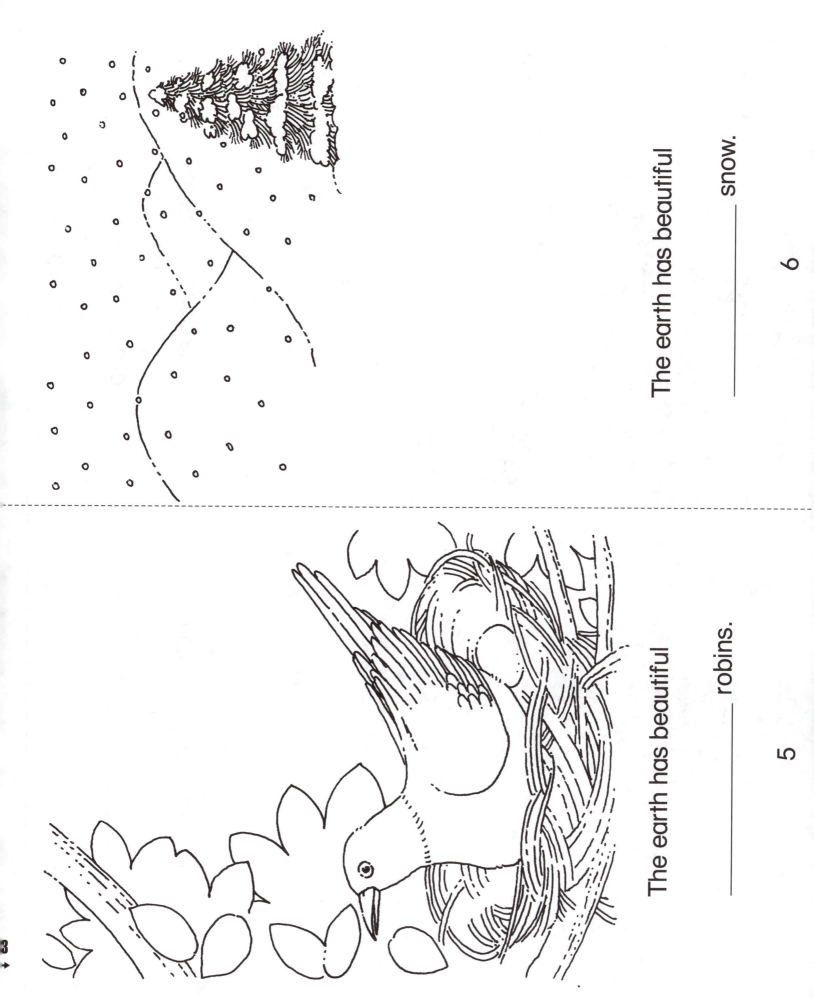

The earth has beautiful
_____ snow.

6

The earth has beautiful
_____ robins.

5

Month-by-Month Write & Read Books Scholastic Professional Books

All the colors make the
earth beautiful.
I love the earth, my home.

8

The earth has a beautiful
_____ sun.

7

It's Springtime!

by _____

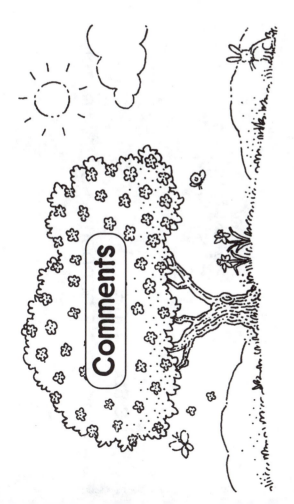

Comments

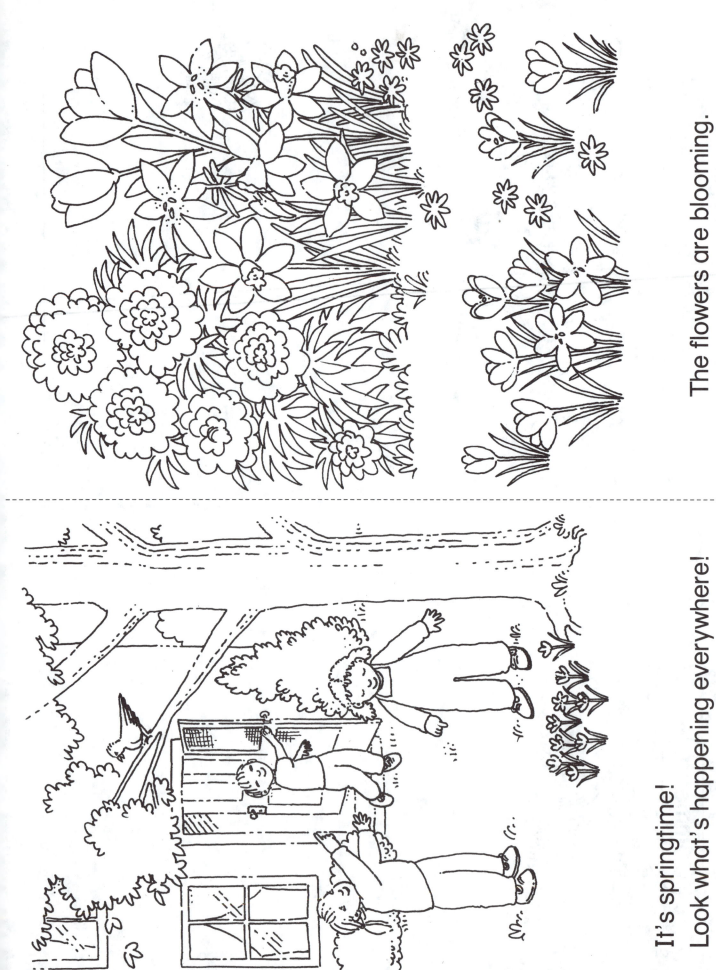

The flowers are blooming.

2

It's springtime!
Look what's happening everywhere!

1

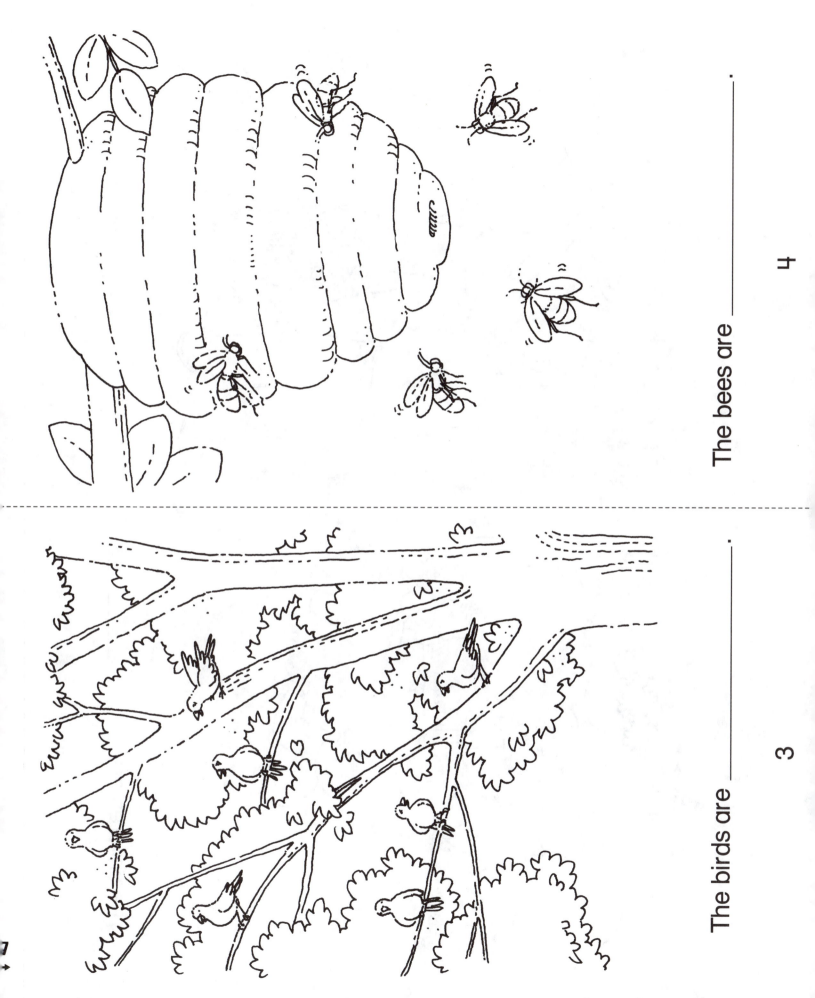

The bees are _____ .

4

The birds are _____ .

3

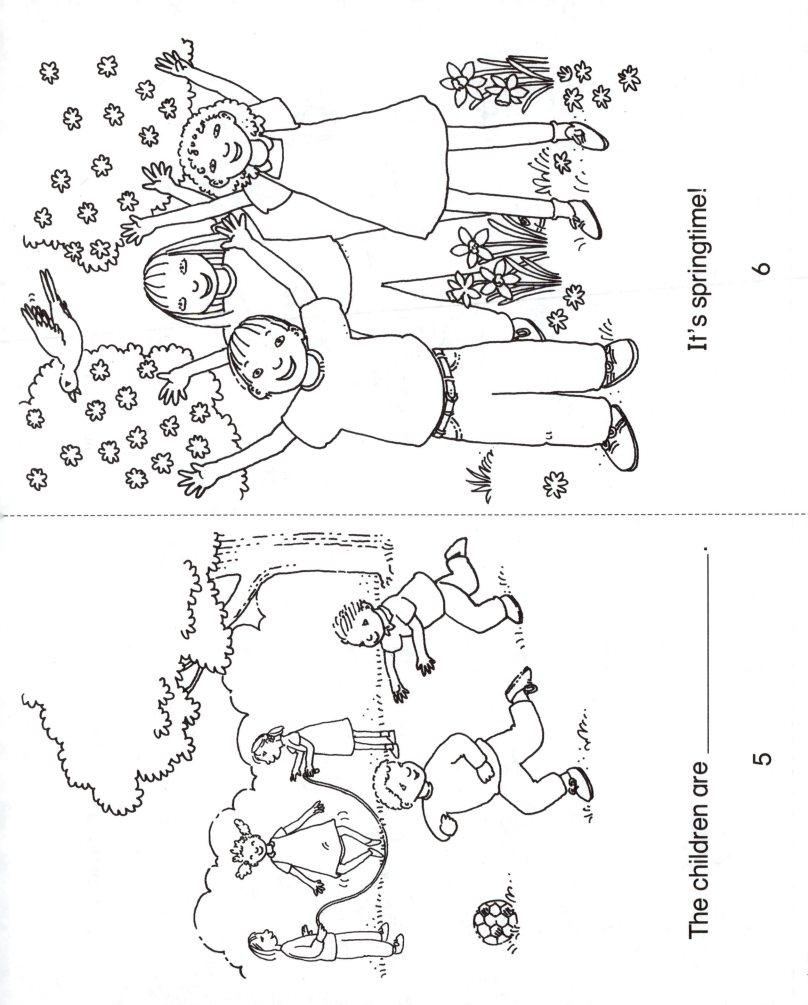

It's springtime!

6

The children are _____.

5

Month-by-Month Write & Read Books Scholastic Professional Books

My Memory Book

by _____

Month-by-Month Write & Read Books Scholastic Professional Books

Autographs

My teacher's name was

_____.

2

My first day in _____

was _____.

1

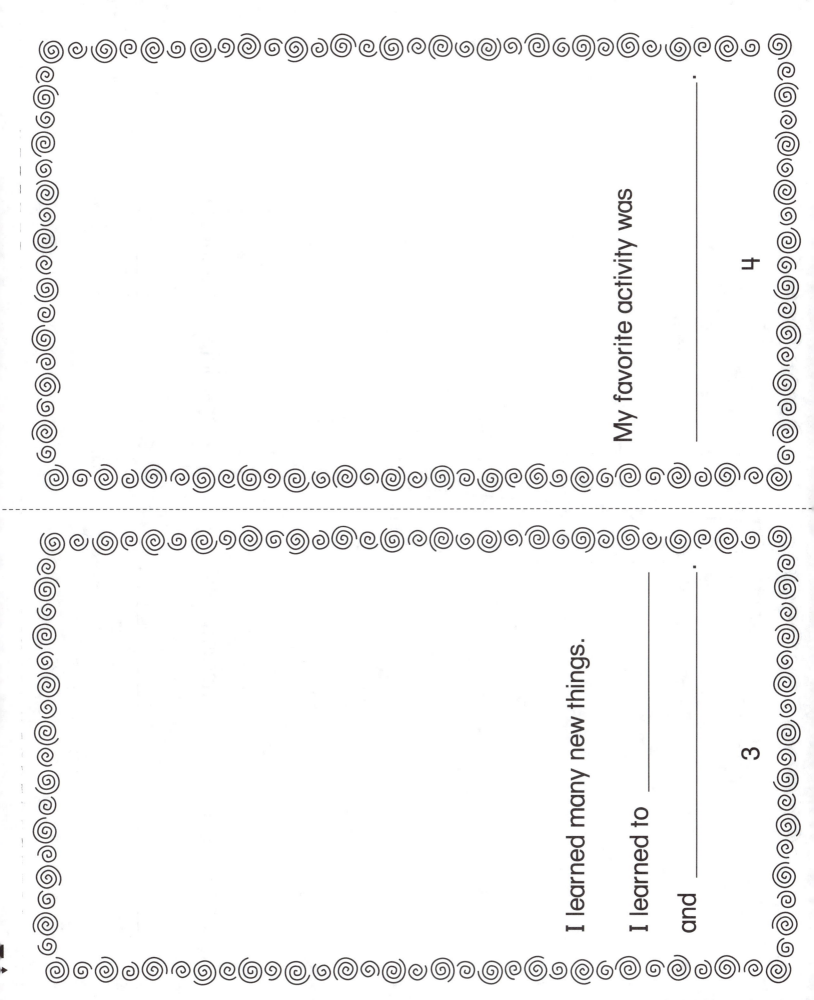

My favorite activity was

_____.

4

I learned many new things.

I learned to _____

and _____.

3

A special event that we celebrated

was _____.

6

I had a special friend named

_____.

5

We had a great year in

_____

8

Some special teachers and
helpers in our classroom were

_____

_____

_____

7

About the Author

This author of this book is _____.

_____ is _____ years old

and lives in _____.

The author likes to _____,

_____, and

_____.

This is a picture of the author,

_____

by _____

Comments